Your Guidebook
to Growing
a Family Economy
Workbook

By Dana Susan Beasley

AngelARTS
A Creative Arts Agency
& Publishing House

Colorado Springs, Colorado

Table of Contents

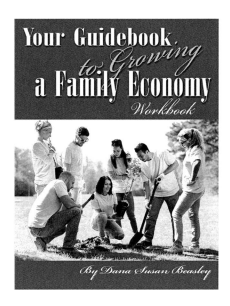

Welcome and Instructions

How to Use this Family Economy Curriculum Workbook

A Creative Arts Agency
& Publishing House

Welcome!

Congratulations on taking a big step for you and your family! I am excited to bring you this workbook that will transform all of your lives!

This is the workbook that corresponds to *Your Guidebook to Growing a Family Economy Manual.*

The workbook contains general questions, vocabulary words, journaling, sketching, planning, and researching. You can use any of these sections for discussion amongst your family, especially as part of school. These would also make great essay questions.

Also, you can use this curriculum and workbook as a springboard to different areas of study. For instance, if you want to teach your child about math, you can have your child keep track of stock prices. This would also easily lead to a course like Consumer Math. I will have ideas periodically throughout the workbook for you and your family to engage in further study.

For some of the assignments you may want to use a handy program like Pinterest to collect your "swipe" file. You also may want to paste pictures you collect into the workbook. Or you may want to create the pictures on your computer, print them out, and then paste them in the workbook.

Some of the exercises will require you to go to a Website to answer the questions. I always make sure the Websites are safe, but it's a good idea to check it out for yourself first beforehand.

I have also included optional "For Further Study" sections. Some of the vocabulary requires research by your student.

If you are in a class or group setting, you can buy in bulk volume on my site. Or you can buy a digital version of the workbook for multiple members of the family.

For more information, go to GrowMyEconomy.com.

At the end of each lesson, I have included an actionable assignment sheet with a place to check off your work. The vocabulary is optional, a handy feature for further learning for teens.

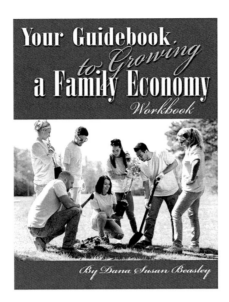

Introduction

Why a Family Economy
and What is it?

A Creative Arts Agency
& Publishing House

General Questions

1 Why do you want to start a business?

_____

_____

_____

_____

2 What are the obstacles holding you back?

_____

_____

_____

_____

3 What are the reasons for having a family economy?

_____

_____

_____

_____

4 What is the history of work? What does God set up in the Garden of Eden in Genesis?

_____

_____

_____

_____

5 Study the passage in Proverbs 31, the passages in Deuteronomy that talk about prosperity, and Ephesians 4. What do you think it's saying about the role of men and women and children in families?

_____

_____

_____

_____

_____

6 Read Ephesians 2:10. The Greek word for workmanship is "poema." How are we like God's masterpieces, His poems?

_____

_____

_____

_____

_____

7 How does the lack of faith hurt your dreams? What is the role of faith in being an entrepreneur?

_____

_____

_____

_____

_____

8 Read Gideon, the story of Abraham leaving Ur to follow God into an unknown country, Joseph who became second-in-command to Pharoah, and how the Israelites cross the Jordan River. How is faith played out in each of these stories and how can you and your children practice faith in your daily life?

_____

_____

_____

_____

_____

9 Read the Parable of the Talents. What do you want God to say to you when you meet Him face to face? How are you burying talents versus investing in them?

_____

_____

_____

_____

10 What is your plan for achieving your dreams and reaching your goals?

_____

_____

_____

_____

_____

11 What actions do you need to take to make it happen?

_____

_____

_____

_____

12 Plan out your multiple streams of income.

_____

_____

_____

_____

_____

Assignment

◯ 1) Get a three-ring binder to contain all your lessons. Put some extra paper— blank, lined, and perhaps graph paper—for notetaking, sketching, and journaling.

◯ 2) Answer the questions on Pages 8–11 in the workbook. If you want to write more than the space provided, include it in your binder.

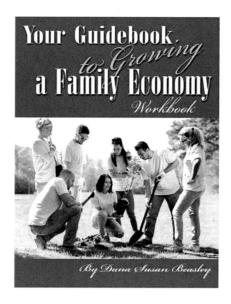

Your Guidebook to Growing a Family Economy Workbook

By Dana Susan Beasley

Lesson 1: How to Start

The Basic Business Building Steps

A Creative Arts Agency
& Publishing House

General Questions

1 What are some "a ha" moments you've had?

_____

_____

_____

_____

2 What is something fun and completely out of the ordinary that you want to do?

_____

_____

_____

_____

3 What do you need to let go of in order for your family economy to move forward?

_____

_____

_____

_____

4 Who are some mentors who can help you and your children?

_____

_____

_____

_____

_____

5 How do you feel when someone serves you to the utmost of your satisfaction?

_____

_____

_____

_____

_____

6 What kind of legal structure do you think you will use?

_____

_____

_____

_____

7 What phone service and mailing address service will you use?

_____

_____

_____

_____

8 What email marketing service will you use?

_____

_____

_____

_____

_____

9 Why are brands important?

_____

_____

_____

_____

_____

The Basic Building Steps Checklist

○ 1 *Thoroughly analyze the following: what's your passion?*

○ 2 *Choose one of these passions and consider business start-up ideas.*

○ 3 *Once you have selected your business concept, ask yourself who your target market would be.*

○ 4 *When you have gathered all this information, decide on a name.*

○ 5 *Have a professional photograph taken of yourself.*

○ 6 *Choose an image that represents your business.*

○ 7 *Set up your business systems. Set up your sales funnel process.*

○ 8 *Purchase a domain name for your business.*

○ 9 *For online business, or even if you are a local product or service, sign up with an autoresponder, like Constant Contact or MailChimp.*

○ 10 *Make your marketing plan.*

○ 11 *If you haven't already done so, create a Facebook profile and a Facebook page.*

○ 12 *Develop a blog and gather a following.*

○ 13 *Develop your product or service.*

○ 14 *Make a launch plan and stick to it.*

○ 15 *Launch your product or service.*

Assignment

◯ 1) Answer the questions on Pages 14-16 in the workbook. If you want to write more than the space provided, include it in your binder.

◯ 2) Do the necessary research if you are ready. Talk to a CPA or tax attorney. Find out what email service you would like to use. Discover what kind of mentors you have around you that could help you and your children.

◯ 3) Use the checklist on Page 17 to help you in each step of starting your business.

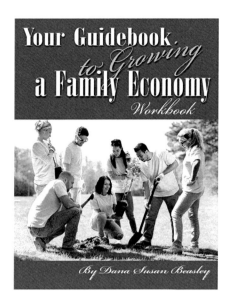

Lesson 2: Building Block One

Create a Vision
of Your
Family Economy

A Creative Arts Agency
& Publishing House

General Questions

1 Why is it important to know your "why?"

_____

_____

_____

_____

2 What makes for an effective brand?

_____

_____

_____

_____

3 The origin of "passion" has Christian theology tied to it, specifically connoting suffering. How does that tie in with the kind of passion this section talks about?

_____

_____

_____

_____

Vocabulary

$\mathcal{W}$rite in the definitions to these vocabulary words.

Mission:

_____

_____

_____

_____

Vision:

_____

_____

_____

_____

Values:

_____

_____

_____

_____

Callings:

_____

_____

_____

_____

_____

Passion:

_____

_____

_____

_____

_____

Dreams:

_____

_____

_____

_____

_____

Goals:

_____

_____

_____

_____

Talents:

_____

_____

_____

_____

Gifts:

_____

_____

_____

_____

Skills:

_____

_____

_____

For Further Study

◯ 1   Research how to write a business plan and create one.

◯ 2   Work on financials for math: revenue projections, cash flow analysis, cost/benefit analysis, etc.

◯ 3   Learn how to use spreadsheet software, like Excel. This is a very important skill to have, especially as an entrepreneur.

Identity Questions

*A*nswer to the best of your ability. Have each family member answer.

1 **What are your life experiences?** Write a story about an accomplishment that had a profound impact on your life. You can write more than one if you like. After you write the story or stories, how do these accomplishments translate to skills and talents that you uniquely possess?

_____

_____

_____

_____

_____

_____

_____

_____

_____

_____

_____

_____

_____

_____

2 What do you value? What are your guiding principles in life and in business? What is important to you? Not important to you?

_____

_____

_____

_____

_____

3 What skills have you acquired? Be sure to use *action* verbs.

_____

_____

_____

_____

_____

4 What are your gifts? What are your talents?

_____

_____

_____

_____

5 What are your *spiritual* gifts? (Spiritual gifts come from God to followers of Christ through the Holy Spirit and are for the common good. Although these gifts are for the building up of the church, I believe it's an important factor in finding out who you are and what you are called to be.) You can take an online spiritual gifts test at:
http://www.kodachrome.org/spiritgift/

This site also has a test for youth so that's pretty exciting!

_____

_____

_____

_____

_____

_____

6 What is your personality type? (This will help you make key decisions, like what work environment helps you to be the most productive, structured or flexible? You can take a Myers-Briggs test here. For a free version, go to this site: https://www.mbticomplete.com/en/index.aspx.)

_____

_____

_____

_____

_____

_____

7 Do you or your children have any special needs or challenges you need to be aware of? For instance, if you are allergic to perfume, you probably don't want to market to perfume users! Are you dyslexic, ADHD, etc.? Do you have a child who has Autism? What are the obstacles you and your family face and how can you overcome them?

_____

_____

_____

_____

_____

_____

_____

8 What are your goals for your life? What are your dearly held dreams? What are your desires and longings? What are your goals for your business? What is your desired result?

_____

_____

_____

_____

_____

_____

_____

_____

9 What are your goals for the next 20 years? What is your desired result?

_____

_____

_____

_____

_____

_____

_____

_____

10 What are your goals for the next 10 years? Five years? What is your desired result?

_____

_____

_____

_____

_____

_____

_____

11 What are your goals for the next year? What is your desired result?

_____

_____

_____

_____

12 What do you hope to get out of this course?

_____

_____

_____

_____

13 What is the purpose of your life? Of your business? Your family? What is the reason for your existence? For the existence of your business?

_____

_____

_____

_____

_____

14 What is your life's mission? Your business's? Your family's? What is the aim of your life and business? What are your callings?

_____

_____

_____

_____

_____

_____

_____

15 What are you passionate about? What gets your blood going? What motivates you to get out of bed in the morning? What excited thoughts keep you up at night?

_____

_____

_____

_____

_____

_____

_____

_____

_____

16 What is your life's vision? A morbid way to ask this question is to think ahead to your funeral. What do you want people to say about you? That you spent a lot of time in the office? What kind of impact do you want to have on people, especially through your business?

_____

_____

_____

_____

_____

_____

_____

_____

17 What is your business vision? What do you want it to look like? When you think about it in the future, how do you imagine it?

_____

_____

_____

_____

_____

_____

18 What are your strengths? What are you good at?

_____

_____

_____

_____

19 What are your weaknesses? What are you not so good at?

_____

_____

_____

_____

20 Now that you've gone through all these questions, here's the most relevant of all (and I will be asking it again)—what is the number one point/message you want to communicate with a new brand/logo image?

_____

_____

_____

_____

_____

Assignment

○ 1) Answer the general questions.

○ 2) (Optional) Write in the vocabulary definitions.

○ 3) (Optional) Do the activities in the For Further Study section.

○ 4) Answer the 20 questions in this lesson. If you want to write more than the space provided, include it in your binder.

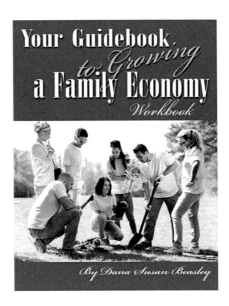

Your Guidebook to Growing a Family Economy Workbook

By Dana Susan Beasley

Lesson 3: Building Block Two

Definitions You Must Know to Get Started

A Creative Arts Agency
& Publishing House

General Questions

1 Why is strategic branding so important?

_____

_____

_____

_____

2 What's the difference between a brand and a slogan?

_____

_____

_____

3 What causes a prospect to click on one image over another?

_____

_____

_____

Notice the brands you use on a daily basis. What drew you to that brand? What emotions does that brand bring across to you? Are you loyal to that brand?

_____

_____

_____

_____

_____

_____

_____

_____

_____

_____

_____

_____

_____

_____

_____

_____

_____

Vocabulary

_W_rite in the definitions to these vocabulary words.

Logo:

_____

_____

_____

_____

Identity:

_____

_____

_____

_____

Brand:

_____

_____

_____

Slogan:

_____

_____

_____

_____

Trademark:

_____

_____

_____

_____

Branding Strategy:

_____

_____

_____

_____

Identity Collateral:

_____

_____

_____

_____

Assignment

◯ 1) Answer the general questions.

◯ 2) (Optional) Write in the vocabulary definitions.

◯ 3) Collect pictures of your favorite brands. Your snail mailbox is a great source for this! Direct mailers really know how to market! Start a file for your favorite images, including logos/brands you find online, in your home, and in your mailbox. What is it about the brand that appeals to you? What message does it get across? What colors does it use? What images or symbols? Observe closely! For your convenience, you can collect these in a clear envelope for your notebook.

   If you Pinterest, this is a great tool to make your "swipe" file!

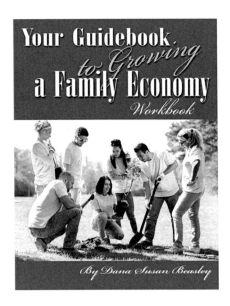

Lesson 4: Building Block Three

Persona Vs. Name: Which One Are You?

A Creative Arts Agency
& Publishing House

General Questions

1 Why is choosing a name an important factor in creating your brand?

_____

_____

_____

_____

2 What makes for a good name?

_____

_____

_____

_____

3 What are the differences between a persona and personal name brand?

_____

_____

_____

_____

4 What are the pros and cons of persona brands?

_____

_____

_____

_____

5 What are the pros and cons of personal name brands?

_____

_____

_____

_____

6 What are examples you can find that are persona brands? What appeals to you about them? Is it effective? What is the brand's drawbacks? What emotions/associations does it bring up? How effective does their logo reflect their persona?

_____

_____

_____

_____

_____

_____

_____

_____

_____

_____

_____

7 What are examples you can find of personal name brands? Notice brands named after specific people. How effective is the logo? Would you remember the person? What emotions does the brand communicate?

_____

_____

_____

_____

_____

_____

_____

_____

_____

_____

§ When is it time to change a name?

_____

_____

_____

_____

_____

§ Why is it important for company reps and direct sellers to have brands?

_____

_____

_____

_____

_____

_____

_____

_____

_____

_____

Vocabulary

$\mathcal{W}$rite in the definitions to these vocabulary words.

Persona:

_____

_____

_____

Bankruptcy:

_____

_____

_____

Promise:

_____

_____

_____

Disconnect:

_____

_____

_____

Your Choices

*W*rite below the decisions you will make after working on this lesson.

Now it's your turn to decide. Are you going to name your business a persona or after your own name? Which one will you be?

_____

_____

_____

_____

_____

_____

_____

_____

_____

_____

_____

_____

Note: You are not stuck to this decision. It's just part of the brainstorming process!

Assignment

○ 1) Answer the general questions.

○ 2) (Optional) Write in the vocabulary definitions.

○ 3) Make an INITIAL decision about which way you want to go, based on the above research. Write it down on Page 47. You can always change as we go through the lessons, but this will help you in your brainstorming as you gather more information and start making some concrete decisions.

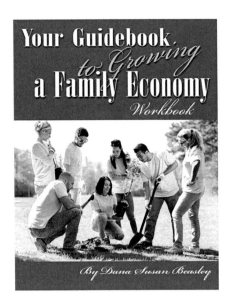

Lesson 5: Building Block Four

Essential Elements of a Well-Designed Logo/Brand

A Creative Arts Agency
& Publishing House

General Questions

1 Why is understanding the elements important in designing your brand image? What is the benefit?

_____

_____

_____

_____

2 How will knowing the process of design help you if you decide to hire a graphic designer?

_____

_____

_____

_____

3 What are the two components of a logo?

_____

_____

_____

_____

4 What is a big mistake many business owners make when it comes to typography?

_____

_____

_____

_____

5 What is the most important factor when choosing elements for your logo?

_____

_____

_____

_____

6 What are the three basic types of typography?

_____

_____

_____

7 Why is it a good idea to use a photograph of yourself?

_____

_____

_____

_____

8 What is the resolution you need to use for print? For Web?

_____

_____

9 What are the different types of color?

_____

_____

10 Why isn't spot color used much these days? What is it used for?

_____

_____

11 How does paper effect a design?

_____

_____

12 Why is color important in design?

_____

_____

Vocabulary

*W*rite in the definitions to these vocabulary words.

Typography:

_____

Logomark:

_____

Element:

_____

Contrast:

_____

Balance:

_____

Composition:

_____

Proportion:

_____

Aestheticism:

_____

_____

Weight:

_____

_____

Tone:

_____

_____

Spacing:

_____

Fonts:

_____

Illustrations:

_____

_____

Lighting:

_____

_____

Angle:

_____

_____

Resolution:

_____

_____

RGB:

_____

Web Safe Colors:

_____

_____

CMYK:

_____

_____

Spot Color:

_____

_____

Grayscale:

_____

_____

For Further Study

○ 1 Visit an offset printer and a digital printer. Learn about plates, film, and ink technology. Consider shadowing (have your teen or college student go to work with them) one of these professions for a day.

○ 2 Visit a silk screener or embroiderer. Consider shadowing.

○ 3 Write a paper on the history of printing and media.

Your Vision

*N*ow that I've given you a broad view of the elements of your brand, begin envisioning what that brand would look like.

What kind of typography will you use for your brand name? What image will you use for your logomark, if any? An illustration, a computer drawing, a photograph?

Draw a preliminary sketch below. It doesn't have to be perfect. You are not stuck with it. You are just trying to get an initial creative concept to get the ideas flowing. You will have more opportunities in later lessons to refine your vision and make it into a strategy.

Assignment

○ 1) Answer the general questions.

○ 2) (Optional) Write in the vocabulary definitions.

○ 3) (Optional) Choose some activities from the For Further Study section.

○ 4) Keep collecting brands you like and you don't like. What fonts are used? What images? Are they computer drawings? Illustrations? Photographs? How complicated are these brands?

○ 5) Draw an initial sketch on Page 57.

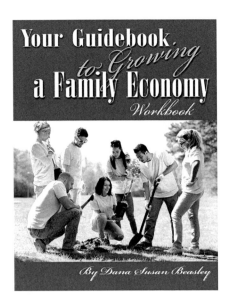

Lesson 6: Building Block Five

The Best Software
to Build Your Brand

A Creative Arts Agency
& Publishing House

General Questions

1 What kind of equipment do you and your family think you need to purchase?

_____

_____

_____

2 What is the best software for designing logos?

_____

_____

_____

3 Why is it best to get demos before you buy?

_____

_____

_____

4 Why isn't it a good idea to design in Microsoft Word?

_____

_____

Vocabulary

*W*rite in the definitions to these vocabulary words.

Scanner:

_____

_____

Drum Scanner:

_____

_____

Vector Art:

_____

_____

PDF:

_____

_____

A Cloud Service:

_____

_____

For Further Study

◯ 1   Take a class on one of the software programs that you or your children want to learn more about.

Your Software Choices

I've shared a lot of information about software programs. Now it's your turn to research.

In the columns below, write your top three choices for each category after you thoroughly research the programs and what they have to offer.

Professional	Moderately Priced	Free

Assignment

○   1)   Answer the general questions.

○   2) (Optional) Write in the vocabulary definitions.

○   3) (Optional) Choose some activities from the For Further Study section.

○   4) Research the software program choices I highlighted in this lesson. Fill out the form on Page 63, writing down your top three choices in each category. Remember that many of the applications that cost money offer a free demo.

○   5) Decide which program you will use. If it is a paid version, download the demo. If it is a free version, download the software. If it is a cloud service, sign up for it.

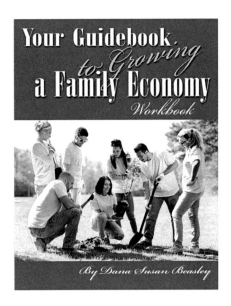

Lesson 7: Building Block Six

Generate Ideas that Spark Your Creativity

A Creative Arts Agency
& Publishing House

General Questions

1 Why is creativity important?

_____

_____

_____

_____

_____

_____

2 How can we see God's creativity all around us?

_____

_____

_____

_____

_____

_____

_____

3 Why is having an imagination when it comes to designing logos important?

_____

_____

_____

_____

_____

4 What are your favorite ways to spark creativity?

_____

_____

_____

_____

_____

_____

_____

_____

_____

_____

_____

5 How can you combine business, school, and family time in order to experience and instill creativity?

_____

_____

_____

_____

_____

_____

_____

_____

_____

6 What's stopping you from being creative?

_____

_____

_____

_____

_____

_____

_____

_____

7 How does clutter lead to lack of creativity?

_____

_____

_____

_____

_____

_____

8 What are some ways you can simplify so you have more creativity in your life?

_____

_____

_____

_____

_____

_____

_____

_____

_____

_____

_____

_____

_____

Vocabulary

$\mathcal{W}$rite in the definitions to these vocabulary words.

Create:

_____

_____

_____

Creator:

_____

_____

_____

Creative:

_____

_____

_____

Creativity:

_____

_____

_____

I Will Spark My Creativity By...

*H*ow will you spark your creativity? Choose your favorite three ideas and write them down below. Then go for it!

Creative Idea #1	Creative Idea #2	Creative Idea #3

Assignment

◯   1) Answer the general questions.

◯   2) (Optional) Write in the vocabulary definitions.

◯   3) Choose your favorite three creativity ideas. Write them down on Page 71. Then go for it!

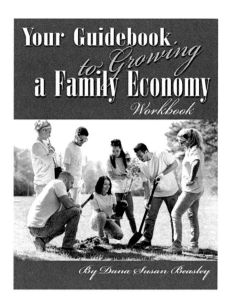

Lesson 8: Building Block Seven

Create a
Brand
Strategy

A Creative Arts Agency
& Publishing House

General Questions

1 What happens if you don't get your brand in front of your target market?

_____

_____

_____

2 What are the three main ways to promote your brand?

_____

_____

_____

3 Why is it important to have a Web presence?

_____

_____

4 What is the key to promoting your brand?

_____

_____

_____

5 What happens when your brand is promoted consistently across all mediums?

_____

_____

_____

_____

6 What are the advantages of automating your marketing?

_____

_____

_____

7 Why is a list important?

_____

_____

_____

_____

8 Where can you distribute your business card?

_____

_____

_____

_____

9 What kind of groups or associations can you get involved in so you develop relationships with your target market?

_____

_____

_____

10 Why shouldn't you just market to friends and family and leave it at that?

_____

_____

_____

11 How would you feel if a friend joined a business, then pressured you to buy from them or get involved, and when you said no she stopped being your friend?

_____

_____

_____

_____

12 How do you think Jesus would want us to treat your target market?

_____

_____

_____

_____

13 What printing materials would be effective for your business?

_____

_____

14 Why is it important to have customer retention programs?

_____

_____

15 What are the advantages to using promotional products?

_____

_____

_____

16 How can you make money from your brand?

_____

_____

_____

17 What are the best formats for using your logo?

_____

_____

_____

Vocabulary

$\mathcal{W}$rite in the definitions to these vocabulary words.

Brand Strategy:

_____

Promotion:

_____

Exposure:

_____

Strategy:

_____

Tactic:

_____

Online and Offline Marketing:

_____

Automation:

_____

List:

_____

Consistency:

_____

Sphere of Influence:

_____

Elevator Speech:

_____

Networking:

_____

Promotional Products:

_____

Print on Demand:

_____

Personalization:

_____

Format:

_____

For Further Study

○ 1 Research how to write a marketing plan and create one.

○ 2 Work on financials for math: marketing costs.

○ 3 If you haven't already done so, learn how to use spread-sheet software, like Excel. This is a very important skill to have, especially as an entrepreneur.

Your Brand Strategy

*C*hoose three or four methods from online, offline, and promotional products marketing methods and write down how you plan on putting it to effect and the frequency with which you plan on using it.

Online	Frequency

Offline	Frequency

Promotional Products	Frequency

Assignment

○ 1) Answer the general questions.

○ 2) (Optional) Write in the vocabulary definitions.

○ 3) (Optional) Choose some activities from the For Further Study section.

○ 4) Choose three or four online, offline, and promotional products marketing methods and write them in the space provided on Page 81. Also include the frequency you plan on doing these activities: daily, weekly, monthly, etc.

○ 5) Translate these activities to your calendar when you are ready to launch your business.

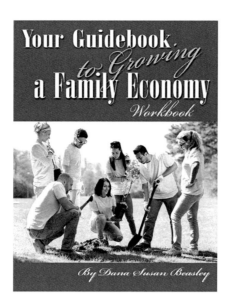

By Dana Susan Beasley

Lesson 9: Building Step One

Collect
Information

A Creative Arts Agency
& Publishing House

General Questions

1 What does finding your identity require?

_____

_____

_____

2 What are the three steps to finding your identity?

_____

_____

_____

3 Why should business owners and entrepreneurs go through this arduous process?

_____

_____

_____

4 How can you discover your new identity?

_____

_____

_____

Vocabulary

Write in the definitions to these vocabulary words.

Process:

_____

_____

_____

Analysis:

_____

_____

_____

Implementation:

_____

_____

_____

Quest:

_____

_____

_____

Image Branding:

_____

_____

_____

Examine:

_____

_____

_____

Collect:

_____

_____

_____

Visual:

_____

_____

_____

Hunt:

_____

_____

_____

For Further Study

○ 1 Research your chosen target market. Who are they? What is their income? Education? What pain are they experiencing? What are they afraid of losing? Where on the Internet can you find them? Where in your region can you find them? What trade magazines and newsletters do they subscribe to?

Your Identity Quest

*T*he following questions will help you gain clearer insight into your business and marketing goals, thus bringing you more success. So, as you embark on this journey of discovering your new brand identity, answer the following questions thoroughly and thoughtfully and to the best of your knowledge.

Project yourself into the future, getting a feel for what your business would be like. Some of these questions may seem like duplicates. Answer them anyway. They are designed to draw more and more specific answers out of you.

We are essentially drilling down into more and more specifics. You started this work in your first lesson, now we are in the process of refining your vision so you can get laser-focus on the best brand for you, a brand that will truly sizzle!

1 | Why do you want to start your business and if you have already started your business, how has it developed?

_____

_____

_____

_____

_____

_____

_____

2 What does your business do well? Not do well?

_____

_____

_____

_____

_____

_____

_____

3 How do you, as a small business, treat vendors, customers, employees? What is your attitude toward your audience or target market?

_____

_____

_____

_____

4 Who is your target market? Who are you in business for? Who is your audience? (Be specific as possible. Even put a picture of your target market on your wall to remind you.)

_____

_____

_____

_____

5 How do employees, vendors, suppliers, and the financial community feel about your business?

_____

_____

_____

_____

6 Who are your important publics? How do you interface with them?

_____

_____

_____

_____

7 How do you want your business to be seen/perceived? How is it perceived by your audience or your target market?

_____

_____

_____

_____

_____

_____

8 What are the benefits to your customers/constituents when a new identity is created for you?

_____

_____

_____

_____

_____

_____

9 Who is your competition?

_____

_____

_____

_____

10 What is your business vision?

_____

_____

_____

_____

_____

11 How does your company's existing graphic identity support your vision?

_____

_____

_____

_____

_____

12 What changes are you trying to affect with this new logo?

_____

_____

_____

_____

_____

_____

_____

13 What are your communication objectives with this new logo/ collateral?

_____

_____

_____

_____

_____

14 Do you have a vision of what the new logo will look like? Feel free to sketch if you like. (You did this in a previous lesson, but it never hurts to draw your ideas multiple times!)

_____

_____

_____

_____

_____

_____

_____

15 What do you feel would be a success for this new logo/brand?

_____

_____

_____

_____

_____

16 What are your marketing objectives with this new logo/brand/collateral?

_____

_____

_____

_____

17 How do you direct people/make people aware of your products or services?

_____

_____

_____

_____

18 What is the volume of marketing you want to do with your new brand identity and any new collateral it is applied to?

_____

_____

_____

_____

_____

19 Who are your current designers/suppliers and what are they doing for you/not doing for you? What are your likes/dislikes of the work they are doing for you?

_____

_____

_____

_____

_____

20 What is the single most important point you want to make with a new brand identity?

_____

_____

_____

_____

_____

_____

Your Visual Quest

*I*f you already have a logo/brand, look at all your Websites, marketing collateral, signage, business cards, brochures, video marketing, social media, etc. If you don't have a brand yet, find a business you look up to, preferably someone in your field. Try to find as much information about them as you can—what does their Website look like, their business cards, brochures, signage... everything you can get your hands on or look at through the Internet or offline. This exercise is also useful to do with your direct and indirect competition.

Ask yourself:

1 Is there consistency between all mediums? For example, does the logo on the business card look the same on the Website, signage, social marketing, brochure, etc.?

_____

_____

_____

2 Look at your brand (or the brand you chose to study if you don't have a brand) from a potential client's perspective. Is there any confusion about what your (or their) business offers? Does it encapsulate the essence of your particular Unique Selling Proposition?

_____

_____

_____

_____

Your Identity Hunt

*W*hether or not you have a brand already, go on a hunt. Collect business cards, observe signage, note Websites you like, look at design books. What kind of style best reflects your business, organization, or artistry personality? Modern? Traditional? Wild? Conservative? Playful? Bold? Daring? Dependable? Find the word or words that is the best description and collect many examples of what you like and don't like. Junk mail is a great source for this research. Don't know where to start? Here are a couple more of my favorite books: *Promo2* by Lauri Miller and *Marketing & Promoting Your Work* by Maria Piscopo.

Use Pinterest to collect your findings! This will make an easy reference for you later on! Or take the family to the library! That always makes for a fun outing!

List your descriptive words below:

_____

_____

_____

_____

_____

_____

_____

_____

_____

Assignment

○ 1) Answer the general questions.

○ 2) (Optional) Write in the vocabulary definitions.

○ 3) (Optional) Do the activity from the For Further Study section.

○ 4) Answer the 20 **Your Identity Quest** questions.

○ 5) Collect all your collateral (or of a business you admire or compete with) and answer the two **Your Visual Quest** questions. your responses on Page 96.

○ 6) Collect as much branding materials as you can, as described in the **Your Identity Hunt** section. Keep a file and refer to it often. Use Pinterest if you prefer. Even take photographs of different signage and print them out for your reference or pin them. Enter in descriptive words that describe your business.

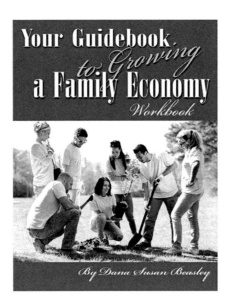

By Dana Susan Beasley

Lesson 10: Building Step Two

Name Your
Company

A Creative Arts Agency
& Publishing House

General Questions

1 What do words contain and what do they convey?

_____

_____

_____

2 How does knowing that help in designing a logo?

_____

_____

_____

3 When should you change a name of a business?

_____

_____

_____

4 Where do you apply your name?

_____

_____

_____

5 How do you come up with business name ideas?

_____

_____

_____

_____

_____

6 Why is doing keyword research helpful?

_____

_____

_____

_____

_____

7 What do you need to keep in mind when naming your business?

_____

_____

_____

_____

_____

8 What are some strategies to choosing your name?

_____

_____

_____

_____

9 What do you do once you have selected a few possibilities of names?

_____

_____

_____

_____

10 What are the legalities of naming your company?

_____

_____

11 How do you register a domain name and why is it important?

_____

_____

_____

Vocabulary

_W_rite in the definitions to these vocabulary words.

Convey:

_____

_____

Connotation:

_____

_____

Association:

_____

_____

Brand Equity:

_____

_____

Keywords:

_____

_____

Thesaurus:

_____

Mindmap:

_____

Criteria:

_____

Trademark:

_____

DBA:

_____

LLC:

_____

Sole Proprietorship:

_____

Domain:

_____

Hosting Company:

_____

For Further Study

○ **1** Research what a patent, trademark, and copyright is.

○ **2** Study business law.

The Why of Your Name

*B*elow answer the questions about the name you want to choose for your business.

1 If you chose to use your personal name, write below how you want it to appear:

_____

_____

_____

_____

2 What do you want your company name to convey?

_____

_____

_____

3 What effect do you want it to have on people?

_____

_____

_____

4 What are the strategic goals of your company name?

_____

_____

_____

_____

_____

_____

_____

5 What criteria do you have for your company name?

_____

_____

_____

_____

_____

_____

_____

_____

Your Name Choices

*L*ist the names you have brainstormed for your business. Then put them in order of preference.

Favorites	Why	Least Favorites	Why?
_____	_____	_____	_____
_____	_____	_____	_____
_____	_____	_____	_____
_____	_____	_____	_____
_____	_____	_____	_____
_____	_____	_____	_____
_____	_____	_____	_____
_____	_____	_____	_____
_____	_____	_____	_____
_____	_____	_____	_____
_____	_____	_____	_____
_____	_____	_____	_____
_____	_____	_____	_____
_____	_____	_____	_____
_____	_____	_____	_____
_____	_____	_____	_____
_____	_____	_____	_____

Narrowing the List Down

*N*ow we are getting down to brass tacks. It's time for you to consolidate your name into your top picks. List your top three choices below and answer the following questions:

"What does this name mean to you? What kind of image comes to mind? What kind of company does it sound like? What kind of products do you think a company with this name might make?" (Rose DeNeve)

1 _____
_____
_____
_____

2 _____
_____
_____
_____

3 _____
_____
_____
_____
_____
_____

Drum Roll Please: The Final Choice

*S*o now you've done a lot of hard work: you've analyzed, brainstormed, asked trusted friends and associates their opinion. It's time to make a decision. Write down your top choice below:

1 My name brand choice:

_____

_____

_____

2 Why did I choose it?

_____

_____

_____

3 What is my vision for this name brand?

_____

_____

_____

4 What are my trusted friends/associates opinions of it?

_____

_____

_____

_____

_____

_____

_____

_____

5 Is it available for trademark registration, DBA registration, and domain registration?

_____

_____

_____

_____

_____

_____

_____

_____

_____

Assignment

◯ 1) Answer the general questions.

◯ 2) (Optional) Write in the vocabulary definitions.

◯ 3) (Optional) Do the activities from the For Further Study section.

◯ 4) Answer the questions on Pages 106-107. Start brainstorming a list of possible business names. Keep a notebook with you at all times or use a mindmapping tool. When you have 10-20 names, write them down on Page 108 in order of preference and comment why you like or not like the name so much.

◯ 5) Narrow your list down to the top three choices. Write these down on Page 109. Check with the trademark office, your department of revenue, and GoDaddy to make sure these names are completely available.

◯ 6) Decide on your top name and write it down on Page 110-111. Answer the questions.

◯ 7) What if you decided to use your own name as your brand? Answer the questions on Pages 106-107 and 110-111. Use Page 108 to list in order of preference exactly what part or parts of your name you will use.

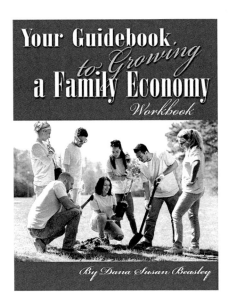

Lesson 11: Building Step Three

Write a Slogan

A Creative Arts Agency
& Publishing House

General Questions

1 Why do you want to have a buzz about your business?

_____

_____

_____

_____

2 What are some slogans that you remember?

_____

_____

_____

_____

3 How do slogans become part of culture? List examples.

_____

_____

_____

_____

_____

4 What is a slogan made of?

_____

_____

_____

_____

5 What are some ways to write a slogan?

_____

_____

_____

_____

6 What do you do after you have written your slogan?

_____

_____

_____

_____

Vocabulary

*W*rite in the definitions to these vocabulary words.

Slogan:

_____

_____

_____

Unique Selling Proposition:

_____

_____

_____

_____

Motto:

_____

_____

Tagline:

_____

_____

_____

Pithy:

_____

_____

_____

Jingle:

_____

_____

_____

Alliteration:

_____

_____

_____

Simile:

_____

_____

_____

Metaphor:

_____

_____

_____

_____

For Further Study

◯ 1 Create a musical jingle and video record it. If you have a YouTube account, upload it.

◯ 2 Write a poem using alliteration, metaphors, and similes.

My Statement of Value

I work with _____ (your target market)

who struggle with _____ (pain your target

market experiences) so that they can experience

_____ (result they get by working with you).

My 60-Second Elevator Pitch

*W*rite your 60-second elevator pitch below. How would you answer this question if you only had a minute: *"What do you do?"*

_____

_____

_____

_____

_____

_____

_____

_____

_____

_____

My 30-Second Elevator Pitch

*W*rite your 30-second elevator pitch below. How would you answer this question if you only had half a minute: *"What do you do?"*

_____

_____

_____

_____

_____

_____

_____

My 10-Second Elevator Pitch

*W*rite your 10-second elevator pitch below. How would you answer this question if you only had 10 seconds: *"What do you do?"*

_____

_____

_____

_____

Keyword Research

*D*o some research online and find some keywords that you could use for your slogan. Write the best ones below:

_____

_____

_____

_____

_____

_____

_____

_____

_____

_____

_____

_____

_____

_____

_____

_____

_____

_____

_____

Your Slogan

*W*rite below your final choices for your slogan. Be sure to check that these slogans are available.

Favorites	Why?	Least Favorites	Why?
_____	_____	_____	_____
_____	_____	_____	_____
_____	_____	_____	_____
_____	_____	_____	_____
_____	_____	_____	_____
_____	_____	_____	_____
_____	_____	_____	_____
_____	_____	_____	_____
_____	_____	_____	_____
_____	_____	_____	_____
_____	_____	_____	_____
_____	_____	_____	_____
_____	_____	_____	_____
_____	_____	_____	_____
_____	_____	_____	_____
_____	_____	_____	_____

Your Top Choice

*W*rite below your final choices for your slogan. Be sure to check that these slogans are available.

_____

_____

_____

_____

_____

_____

_____

_____

_____

_____

_____

_____

_____

_____

_____

_____

_____

_____

Assignment

○ 1) Answer the general questions.

○ 2) (Optional) Write in the vocabulary definitions.

○ 3) (Optional) Do the activities from the For Further Study section.

○ 4) Answer the questions on Page 119. Write your Statement of Value. Write your 60-second elevator pitch. Then on Page 120 write your 30-second and 10-second elevator pitch.

○ 5) Do keyword research for your slogan and write your top picks on Page 121.

○ 6) On Page 122 write some slogans and list them in order of priority. Choose your favorite slogan and write it down on Page 123. Be sure that these slogans are not trademarked already.

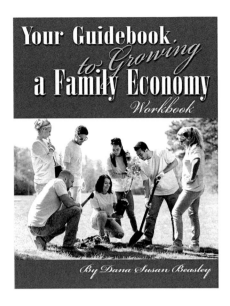

Lesson 12: Building Step Four

Develop a
Design Strategy

A Creative Arts Agency
& Publishing House

General Questions

1 Why is it important to go through this branding process, even if it can be painstaking?

_____

_____

_____

_____

_____

2 What is the key to differentiating yourself from other businesses?

_____

_____

_____

_____

_____

3 What is the importance of knowing your why?

_____

_____

_____

_____

4 What's the difference between self-employment and employment? How can you keep yourself motivated and productive when working for yourself?

_____

_____

_____

_____

_____

5 Why is it important to go through this branding process, even if it can be painstaking?

_____

_____

_____

_____

6 What is your why?

_____

_____

_____

_____

_____

7 What can you say "no" to in order to say "yes" to your dream of creating a family economy?

_____

_____

_____

_____

_____

_____

_____

8 How can you use your time more wisely?

_____

_____

_____

9 What does God say about work and rest?

_____

_____

_____

_____

_____

10 What makes up a successful logo?

_____

_____

_____

_____

_____

_____

_____

_____

_____

11 What are the three criteria for logo design?

_____

_____

_____

_____

_____

_____

_____

_____

Vocabulary

$\mathcal{W}$rite in the definitions to these vocabulary words.

Clarity:

_____

_____

Differentiate:

_____

_____

Communicate:

_____

_____

Credibility:

_____

_____

Initial Concept:

_____

_____

For Further Study

○ 1 Study the passages in the Bible that have to do with work and rest.

○ 2 Go to a trade show or convention and notice all the booths in the vendor hall. What makes one stand out from another? What are your thoughts about a company that has no branding whatsoever?

Your Identity Quest

*S*o, now that I've laid a foundation out for you, here are the specific decisions you need to make regarding your brand. Put a checkmark next to each element you plan to use and then write your criteria for that element below each one.

○ Logomark or symbol (Photograph, illustration, abstract, computer generated art.) Will you even have a logomark? Consider every possibility!

_____

_____

_____

_____

○ Typefaces

_____

_____

_____

_____

○ Color

_____

_____

_____

○ Paper choices (for marketing materials and identity collateral)

_____

_____

_____

○ Backgrounds (this works well with Website banners, business cards, thank you cards, etc)

_____

_____

_____

○ Photo of you

_____

_____

_____

○ Other elements and criteria for your brand based on your analysis:

_____

_____

_____

_____

○ This is an overview of all the different elements that go into designing your brand. In the next lessons, I will break down these elements into concrete steps.

Thumbnail Sketches

*N*ow that you are defining your strategic vision, it's time to do some thumbnail sketches! Just have a little creative fun and go for it!

You can also make initial designs in your software, print them as thumbnails and paste them here. Then you will be able to evaluate your choices.

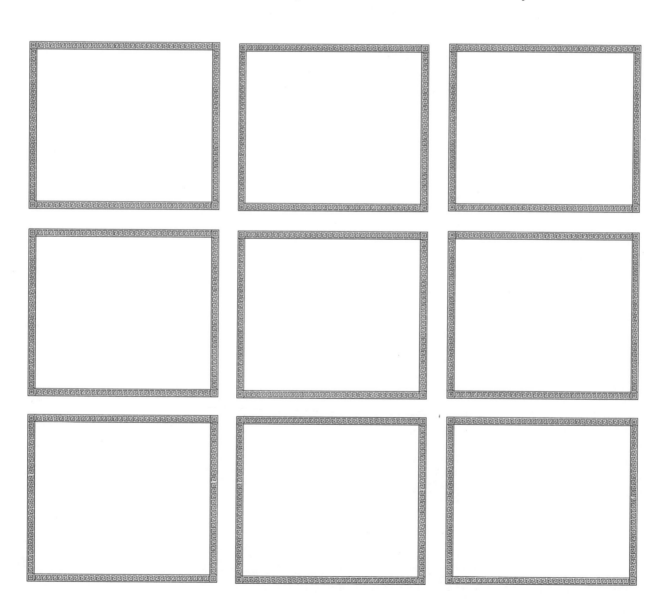

Full Sketch

*N*ow that you've had fun making some initial sketches, do a bigger one. You can copy this page and draw as many times as you want. Or, you can design on software, print it out, and paste here.

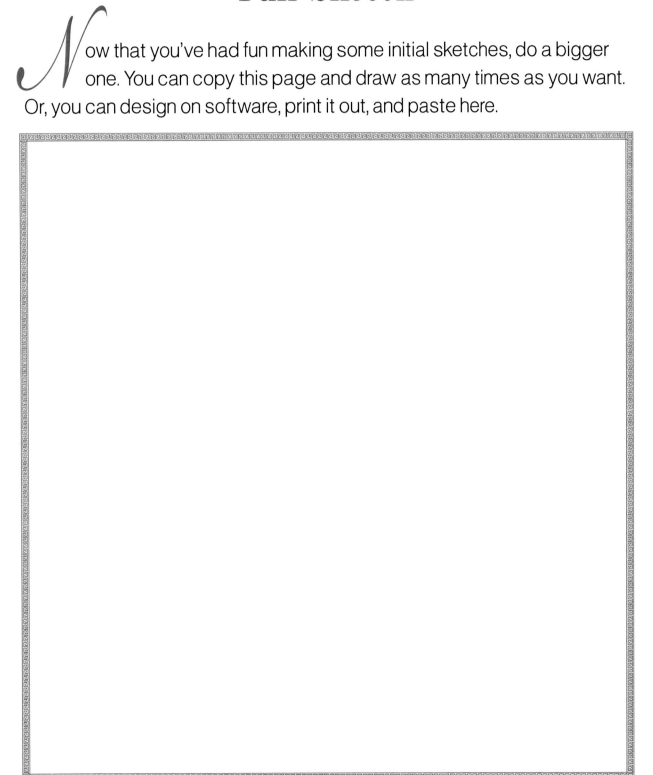

Assignment

○ 1) Answer the general questions.

○ 2) (Optional) Write in the vocabulary definitions.

○ 3) (Optional) Do the activities from the For Further Study section.

○ 4) Analyze and review all the questions you've answered in Lesson 2, 20 questions in Lesson 9, your analysis of existing and name branding material, questions from Lesson 10, and your slogan from Lesson 11. Also, look over your file of favorite brands you have collected for Lesson 3.

○ 5) Answer the questions on Pages 132–133. If you want more room, use your binder.

○ 6) Make initial concept sketches, either with pencil or on your chosen graphic software. Copy the page or draw directly in the workbook. Print out anything you've done on the computer and paste it in the workbook or collect in your binder.

○ 7) Analyze sketches from Page 134 and choose your favorite. Sketch it on Page 135. If you use a computer graphic, print it out and paste it on the sheet.

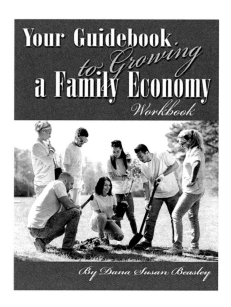

Lesson 13: Building Step Five

Select a
Graphic

A Creative Arts Agency
& Publishing House

General Questions

1 What is the advantage of using FPOs?

_____

_____

_____

_____

2 What do you want to avoid when choosing clip art?

_____

_____

_____

_____

3 Why is it important to make sure you have a license for using images?

_____

_____

_____

_____

4 Why shouldn't you take shortcuts in business?

_____

_____

_____

_____

_____

5 Why should logos be simple?

_____

_____

_____

_____

6 Why does artwork need to be scanned in at high resolution?

_____

_____

_____

7 Why is a good photograph of you important in Internet marketing?

_____

_____

_____

8 How do you get a good photograph?

_____

_____

_____

_____

_____

_____

9 What are some creative ways of creating images for your logo?

_____

_____

_____

_____

_____

_____

_____

_____

_____

Vocabulary

Write in the definitions to these vocabulary words.

Component:

_____

_____

_____

_____

Graphic:

_____

_____

_____

_____

Asset:

_____

_____

_____

_____

FPO:

_____

_____

_____

_____

Royalty Free:

_____

_____

_____

_____

License:

_____

_____

_____

Integrity:

_____

_____

_____

Symbolic:

_____

_____

_____

_____

Drum Scanner:

_____

_____

_____

_____

Flatbed Scanner:

_____

_____

_____

_____

Barter:

_____

_____

_____

_____

For Further Study

◯ 1 Go to an art gallery and experience excellent photography and/or art.

◯ 2 Take a photography or art class. I highly recommend ARTistic Pursuits!

◯ 3 Learn how to do computer illustration via a Web class.

Your Graphic Selections

_D_ecide which kind of graphic you will use: photograph, illustration (or painting), or computer drawing. Write your choice below:

_____

_____

_____

_____

Where will you find your graphic: a stock photography site like **Dreamstime,** a collection of images, do it yourself, or hire someone? Write your choice below:

_____

_____

_____

_____

Who is going to do your personal photograph? What setting will it be taken in? What will you be wearing that will coordinate with your color choices (a whole chapter on color is coming, but just remember that whatever you wear needs to complement your logo, not clash with it). Write your decisions below:

_____

_____

_____

_____

Your Top Choices

*I*f you like, print out your favorite graphics and paste them below. Sometimes having a birds-eye view of your choices helps you to make better decisions.

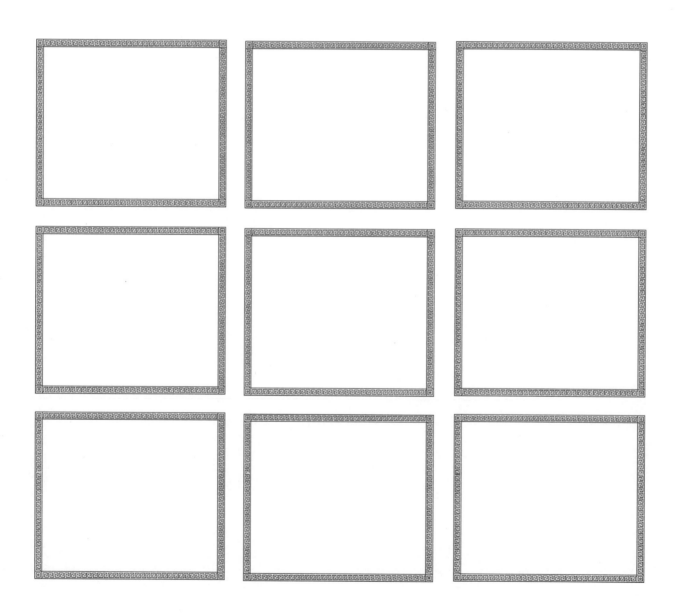

Your Final Choice

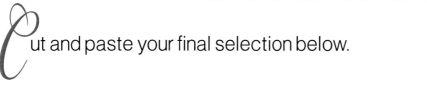

ut and paste your final selection below.

Assignment

○ 1) Answer the general questions.

○ 2) (Optional) Write in the vocabulary definitions.

○ 3) (Optional) Do the activities from the For Further Study section.

○ 4) Answer the questions on Page 145. Choose what kind of graphic you will use. Then choose what source you will select it from: a stock photography site, creating it yourself, or hiring it out. Who will take your personal photograph? Plan what you will wear and what setting it will be taken in.

○ 5) Do research and select your graphic. If you decide to do it yourself, do some sketches and decide what your favorite one is. If you want to hire someone, start the process! When you get a few favorite images, cut and paste them if you want to on Page 146.

○ 6) Before you make your final selection, be sure the image is not trademarked! Download FPOs if you have chosen one from a stock photography site. Scan an image or have it scanned if you have decided to use original art. Get a preliminary sketch from a professional if you choose to hire the graphic out. Select your favorite and if you wish, copy and paste it on Page 147.

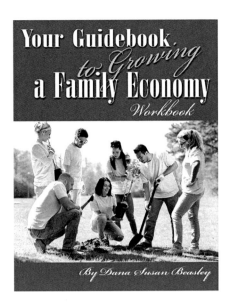

Lesson 14: Building Step Six

Choose Your Colors

A Creative Arts Agency
& Publishing House

General Questions

1 Why is choosing colors important for your brand?

_____

_____

2 What do colors communicate?

_____

_____

3 What do specific color combinations communicate?

_____

_____

4 What is white space and why is it important?

_____

_____

5 What are the characteristics of color?

_____

_____

_____

6 What is a Pantone swatch book used for?

_____

_____

7 How are colors effected by paper?

_____

_____

_____

8 What is the difference between complementary colors and opposite colors?

_____

_____

_____

9 What is the bottom line when choosing colors?

_____

_____

Vocabulary

*W*rite in the definitions to these vocabulary words.

Pantone colors:

_____

Contrast:

_____

Complementary:

_____

Opposite:

_____

Amateur:

_____

Blend:

_____

Gradation:

_____

Tone:

_____

Hue:

_____

Overtone:

_____

Undertone:

_____

Pastel:

_____

Primary:

_____

_____

Trapping:

_____

_____

Pixel:

_____

_____

For Further Study

○ 1   Paint one of the rooms in your house and have fun with color!

○ 2   Take a watercolor or oil painting class and learn all about color!

Your Color Selections

ecide what your color choices are by answering the following:

The mood I want to invoke is: _____

I will choose the color by this method: _____

These are the colors I've chosen: _____

The percentage of these colors are: _____

RGB:
CMYK:
Spot: Pantone _____
Websafe: #_____

RGB:
CMYK:
Spot: Pantone _____
Websafe: #_____

RGB:
CMYK:
Spot: Pantone _____
Websafe: #_____

Assignment

○   1) Answer the general questions.

○   2) (Optional) Write in the vocabulary definitions.

○   3) (Optional) Do the activities from the For Further Study
    section.

○   4) Answer the questions on Page 155. Decide what mood
    you want to communicate with color. Figure out how you
    will find that color, whether through a Pantone swatch book
    or directly clicking on the image you selected. Break down
    the percentages of the colors in RGB, CMYK, spot (if de-
    sired) and Web safe colors.

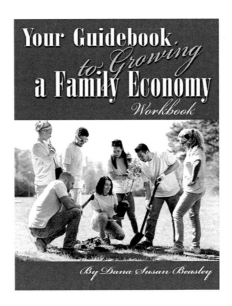

Lesson 15: Building Step Seven

Choose Your Fonts

A Creative Arts Agency
& Publishing House

General Questions

1 By learning about typography, what do you stand to gain?

_____

_____

_____

_____

2 Why are choosing fonts crucial?

_____

_____

_____

_____

3 What are the three basic types of fonts?

_____

_____

_____

_____

4 What are some special effects you can do with fonts?

_____

_____

_____

_____

_____

5 Why do you need to use caps sparingly?

_____

_____

_____

_____

_____

6 What are the three reasons typography is important?

_____

_____

_____

_____

_____

7 What is important when using typography?

_____

_____

_____

_____

_____

8 How can you make your artwork professional using typography?

_____

_____

_____

_____

_____

9 What are the questions you need to ask in order to see words as pictures?

_____

_____

_____

_____

_____

Vocabulary

Write in the definitions to these vocabulary words.

Typography:

_____

_____

Font:

_____

_____

Sans Serif:

_____

_____

Serif:

_____

_____

Leading:

_____

_____

Kerning:

_____

_____

Scale:

_____

_____

Drop Caps:

_____

_____

Indenting:

_____

_____

Baseline:

_____

_____

_____

Smart Quote:

_____

_____

_____

Inch Mark:

_____

_____

Em Dash:

_____

_____

En Dash:

_____

_____

Ellipses:

_____

_____

Caps:

_____

_____

Small Caps:

_____

_____

Pica:

_____

For Further Study

○ 1   Visit a museum that has an old printing press that uses moveable type.

○ 2   Do a stamp art project.

○ 3   Take a course on how to create fonts.

Your Font Selections

 ecide what your font choices are by answering the following:

What is the connotation of my words?

_____

_____

What kind of movement do the words have?

_____

_____

What do the words mean?

_____

_____

What kind of play on words does it have?

_____

My serif choice:

_____

My sans serif choice:

_____

My decorative font choice:

_____

Assignment

○ 1) Answer the general questions.

○ 2) (Optional) Write in the vocabulary definitions.

○ 3) (Optional) Do the activities from the For Further Study section.

○ 4) Answer the questions on Page 165. Imagine what your words look like. See them in a picture. Go exploring in an image manipulation program like Photoshop and choose up to two fonts that capture the essence of your brand identity. If you are really brave, you can choose up to three.

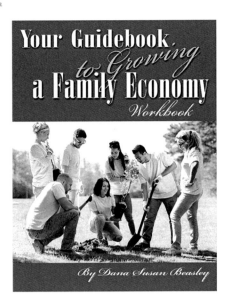

Lesson 16: Building Step Eight

Put It All
Together

A Creative Arts Agency
& Publishing House

General Questions

1 What is the first question to ask yourself when bringing the final design together?

_____

_____

2 What does it mean to line up elements?

_____

3 What minimum resolution do you want to make your logo file?

_____

_____

4 What are the most important things to keep in mind as you design your logo?

_____

_____

5 Why is a backup system so crucial?

_____

_____

Vocabulary

*W*rite in the definitions to these vocabulary words.

Component:

_____

_____

_____

Element:

_____

_____

_____

Shape:

_____

_____

_____

Appealing:

_____

_____

_____

Asymmetrical:

_____

_____

_____

Property:

_____

_____

_____

Emboss:

_____

_____

_____

Feathering:

_____

_____

_____

Ghosted:

_____

_____

_____

For Further Study

1 Study design. What makes a professional one versus an amateur one? Notice how elements are grounded on an axis, how color is used, how balance is obtained, and how contrast is employed.

Your Components

*L*ist below the components for your logo in order of importance.

Number	Components

Your Final Logo

ut and paste your final logo into the space below.

Assignment

○ 1) Answer the general questions.

○ 2) (Optional) Write in the vocabulary definitions.

○ 3) (Optional) Do the activities from the For Further Study section.

○ 4) List your components on Page 172 in order of importance.

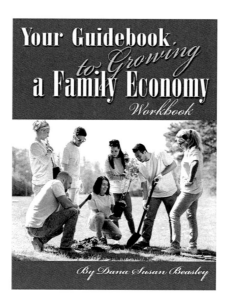

Lesson 17: Building Step Nine

Produce It!

A Creative Arts Agency
& Publishing House

General Questions

1 What are TIFFs used for and what color mode do they need to be in for printing?

_____

_____

2 Why shouldn't you start with a small file and enlarge it?

_____

_____

3 What resolution and color mode are most JPGs set to for Web use?

_____

_____

4 Why is using templates problematic?

_____

_____

5 What are starter files and how do you use them?

_____

_____

6 Why are equidistant, even margins important?

_____

_____

_____

7 Draw the printing triangle.

8 What resolution do you want to make Web banners in?

_____

_____

_____

_____

9 What are some options if you don't want to design your logo yourself?

_____

_____

_____

_____

Vocabulary

*W*rite in the definitions to these vocabulary words.

TIFF:

_____

_____

_____

Mode:

_____

_____

_____

Transparent:

_____

_____

_____

Matte:

_____

_____

_____

Background:

_____

_____

_____

Foreground:

_____

_____

_____

JPEG:

_____

_____

GIF:

_____

_____

Template:

_____

_____

Bleeding:

_____

_____

Trim:

_____

_____

Crop Marks:

_____

_____

Trim Marks:

_____

_____

Gloss:

_____

_____

Freelance:

_____

_____

_____

Ad Agency:

_____

_____

_____

For Further Study

○ 1 Have your student shadow a freelance graphic designer or print broker.

○ 2 Research the technical aspects and history of GIFs, TIFFs, JPEGs, and PDFs.

Your Final Business Card

*C*ut and paste your final business card into the space below.

Your Final Web Banner

*C*ut and paste your final Web banner into the space below.

Assignment

○ 1) Answer the general questions.

○ 2) (Optional) Write in the vocabulary definitions.

○ 3) (Optional) Do the activities from the For Further Study section.

○ 4) Produce your logo into your desired pieces, whether business cards, banners, postcards, or whatever you choose. Just remember to ask for the technical requirements and be sure you produce the file to their standards.

○ 5) Paste your final business card and Web banner onto Page 182.

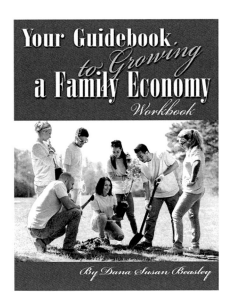

Conclusion

Ready for
the Next Step?

A Creative Arts Agency
& Publishing House

I Would Love to Work With You!

Ready for that next step to make your family economy sizzle? If you want more advanced training or you've decided to hire out the graphic design, why not consider working with someone you know and trust?

Me! Here are some ways you can work with me:

Brand Identity Quest Training Programs

Brand Identity Quest Tutorial Lesson Series

This is all the lessons, plus more! In this 3-month program that comes through your email, you get expanded lessons, bonus lessons on creating marketing plans, business plans, developing content, and much more. You also get a video series where you see how Travis' logo develops.

Enter coupon code FEBIQ for a $20 coupon off of your first month! It includes a free 7-day trial.

Go to BrandIdentityQuest.com for more info!

Creative Genius Services

Creative Logo Designs

Have you completed all your work and just want me to work from your sketch? I will design it for you!

Your Visual Consultation is always free!

After we have our consultation and you send me your completed homework, I can work on your logo!

We are also expanding into Web design in the near future so be sure to check back frequently!

Enter coupon code CSLOGO for a $25 coupon off of your logo service.

Go to AngelArts.biz for more info.

FREE Offers

FREE Strategy Session
5 Secrets to a Wildly Successful Home Business
(wildlysuccessfulhomebusiness.com)
Make Your Brand Sizzle (makeyour-brandsizzle.com)

My Dazzling Future (mydazzlingfuture.com)

Stay connected with me! You can find me on Facebook at AngelArts: A Creative Arts Agency & Publishing House.

Thanks for journeying with me in unmasking your authentic identity! If you would like to be a featured student and show off your work, please contact me! I would love to have your testimonial! And, of course, I will link to your Website! As you apply these lessons learned through this identity quest, I am confident that you will have a brand that sizzles, a future that dazzles, and a growing, thriving family economy!

I look forward to working with you soon and helping you make your family economy brand sizzle and your future dazzle!

Blessings,

Dana

Dana Susan Beasley
Publisher, ***AngelArts***

P.S. You can also call me personally at 719-212-8977 or email me at communications@angelarts.biz. I would be happy to answer any questions you may have.

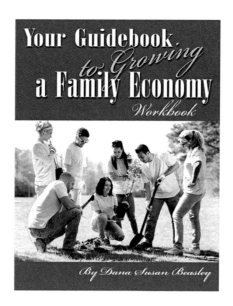

Your Guidebook to Growing a Family Economy
Workbook
By Dana Susan Beasley

About the Author and Publisher

Who is
Dana Susan Beasley
and AngelArts?

A Creative Arts Agency
& Publishing House

About the Author

Dana Susan Beasley is principal/publisher of AngelArts, A Creative Arts Agency & Publishing House. She is passionate about helping families create dazzling futures for themselves by helping them build sizzling brands.

Dedicated to providing excellently-designed ebooks, books, cards, stationery, gifts, and art services to inspirational artists, art enthusiasts, homeschooling families and entrepreneurs, Dana delights in sharing her gifts and talents and the talents of others with people who are passionate about spiritual, personal, educational, professional, ministerial, artistic, and relational growth.

If you like this homeschooling curriculum, you'll love Dana's products and services that will help you reach new heights in your life, home, relationships, homeschooling, business, ministry, and artistry. Her products and services range from unique gifts and cards that will inspire your friends, family, and associates and YOU; to ebooks and books that will transform your life TODAY; to brand marketing and product design courses and services that will make your business stand out above the crowd!

While Dana's expertise is in graphic arts, writing, publishing, and music, she also is a homeschooling mother devoted to working at home. Her desire is that AngelArts, and her work, be a vehicle for God's glory. Because she is always reaching for new heights in her life and beyond and wants to inspire others to do the same!

You can learn more about Dana's products and services at www.AngelArts.biz.

About the Publisher

The mission of *Angel Arts,* A Creative Arts Agency and Publishing House, is to help homeschooling families and the marginalized reach new heights in their lives and beyond through inspirational arts so that they discover God's Callings and become closer to Him.

We do that through inspirational art products, events, and enrichment programs, homeschooling curriculum and resources, and branding, graphics and publishing art services and training.

Why the name AngelArts? Because excellence in art and literature is very important to Dana, and inspirational art is her passion. The company's mission, as Dana envisions it, is to be a vehicle. A vehicle for God's glory, a vehicle for artists to grow in their careers, and a vehicle for her own gifts and talents to grow and help others in publishing, graphic arts, writing, and music.

Dana chose the name AngelArts because ever since she was a little girl she has been reaching for the arts. Her mother, Ann Neal, took this photograph of her when she was a toddler, complete with tinsel halo above her head. She was always reaching for the piano, Mrs. Neal says, and wanted to learn from a young age. She finally was able to get lessons at age seven and is still playing (when time and homeschooling duties allow) on the same piano years later!

If you liked this devotional, you will love Dana's live presentations! She is available on a limited basis to speak at women's groups, networking groups, retreats, and churches. Her presentation, *3 Biblically-Based Fool-Proof Strategies that Will Transform Your Stress into Blessings,* can also include her singing and playing original songs on piano and guitar.

Thank you for taking the time to read this book! Together we can reach new heights in our lives and beyond!

Made in the USA
San Bernardino, CA
13 April 2018